bootleg bakery

bootleg bakery

wickedly boozy treats inspired by the roaring twenties

KIKI BEE

photography by William Lingwood

rps

LONDON • NEW YORK

To the wonderful flappers in my life with whom I have shared love,
laughter and inappropriate amounts of hooch and cake.
Thanks Ma, Lisa, Aimée, Viv and Angela.

Designer Paul Stradling
Photographic Art Direction Sonya Nathoo
Editor Rebecca Woods
Production Manager Toby Marshall
Art Director Leslie Harrington
Editorial Director Julia Charles

Indexer Hilary Bird
Food Stylist Lucy McKelvie
Food Stylist Assistant Ellie Jarvis

First published in 2013 by
Ryland Peters & Small
20–21 Jockey's Fields
London WC1R 4BW
and
519 Broadway, 5th Floor
New York, NY 10012

www.rylandpeters.com

10 9 8 7 6 5 4 3 2 1

Text © Kerry Beeden 2013
Design & photographs © Ryland Peters & Small 2013

ISBN: 978-1-84975-347-0

A CIP record for this book is available from the British Library.

US Library of Congress cataloging-in-Publication Data has been
applied for

Printed in China

NOTES

• All spoon measurements are level, unless otherwise
specified.

• Eggs used in this book are UK Medium, US Large.

• Ovens should be preheated to the specified
temperatures. All ovens work slightly differently.
We recommend using an oven thermometer and
suggest you consult the maker's handbook for any
special instructions, particularly if you are using a
fan-assisted/convection oven, as you will need to
adjust temperatures according to the manufacturer's
instructions.

CONTENTS

WELCOME TO THE BOOTLEG BAKERY

Picture the scene: it's 1929 and a bright young thing is tapping two slows, two quicks, two slows. But this is no gin palace, this is the door of a bakery. He greets the owner with a million dollar smile and slides over a crisp dollar. 'Make mine a cupcake, a dozen of your strongest.' She smiles and places twelve gentile-looking cakes in a box and wraps it with ribbon. The man walks towards the door, turns, blows her a kiss; 'Kiki Bee - you're quite a gal!'

I'm just a girl who can't say no - to a little liquor that is! And in these crazy Prohibition times, we sassy flappers have to get creative. So no gin in teacups for us; if we're going to Sing Sing let's do it in style: cocktail in one hand and cupcake in the other.

What you'll find in the following pages is a selection of my favourite decadent treats. A true Hollywood marriage of cocktail and cake with plenty of zing and dazzle. With the alcohol content high, I've tried to keep the instructions as simple as possible, but there are a few optional fiddly twiddles for those shameful sober types amongst you.

A great cocktail is about two things: quality ingredients and imagination. So splash out a little on the best hooch, the finest chocolate or whatever else the recipe hollers for. Your taste buds will thank you. As for the imagination part, run wild kids! These are recipes that I've shimmied and sashayed to make my own, but I give you a free pass to swirl and shake them into your own concoctions. Who knows what will happen if you swap rum for bourbon, cherries for strawberries, good intentions for naughty ones.

So, all you swinging jazzsters who are ready to cook up a different kind of storm, come and Charleston with me through my secret collection of adult-only recipes. Sugar shakers at the ready!

Love and maraschino cherries,

Kiki Bee x

CHARLESTON COCONUT BLISS

100 g/generous 1 cup desiccated/shredded coconut

100 ml/6½ tablespoons coconut liqueur (such as Malibu)

150 g/1 stick plus 2 tablespoons unsalted butter, softened

100 g/½ cup caster/white sugar

3 eggs, beaten

150 g/1 cup plus 2½ tablespoons self-raising flour

a pinch of salt

1 teaspoon baking powder

FOR THE FILLING

2 very ripe mangoes

freshly squeezed juice of 1 lemon

freshly squeezed juice of 1 lime

50 ml/3½ tablespoons dark rum

FOR THE TOPPING

300 g/2½ cups icing/confectioners' sugar

a sprinkle of coconut flakes

lemon and lime zest (taken from the squeezed lemon and lime in the filling)

2 x 18-cm/7-inch shallow cake pans, lined and greased

SERVES 8–10

BOOZE RATING

You may recognize this as a take on a Victoria Sponge, but let me tell you, fellas, one mouthful of this and you won't remember that dame Victoria. You'll be dreaming of white beaches, azure skies and rum cocktails. If you're not a mango lover, feel free to substitute for a tropical fruit of your choice: passion fruit is lovely and pineapple can give you a real Caribbean hit.

Preheat the oven to 190°C (375°F) Gas 5. Put the desiccated/shredded coconut and coconut liqueur in a bowl and give it a good stir.

In a separate mixing bowl, cream together the butter and sugar until light and fluffy. Add the beaten egg, a little at a time, folding through thoroughly between each addition. Sift the flour, salt and baking powder onto the mixture and, thoroughly but gently, fold all the ingredients together. Finally, add the desiccated coconut and coconut liqueur to the mix and give it a few more gentle stirs.

Divide the mixture between the prepared cake pans and bake in the preheated oven for about 25–30 minutes, until a skewer inserted into the middle of the cakes comes out clean. Allow the cakes to cool completely on a wire rack.

Once the cakes are cool, make the filling. Peel the mangoes and remove the pits. Thinly slice one of the mangoes and set aside. Chop the other mango roughly and put in a bowl. With the back of a fork, mash the mango to a chunky purée, then add the lemon and lime juice and the dark rum and give it a good stir. Spread the mango purée over one of the cakes, then lay the mango slices on top and sandwich with the other cake.

To make the topping, put the icing/confectioners' sugar in a bowl and add enough cold water – a teaspoon at a time – to make a thick, spreadable paste. Spread the icing over the cake, then sprinkle the lemon and lime zest and the coconut flakes over the top. Leave the icing to set before serving.

a cocktail of cakes

COMRADE CAKE

1 tablespoon instant coffee granules

1 teaspoon boiling water

1 teaspoon vodka, plus 1 tablespoon for drizzling

1 teaspoon Kahlúha, plus 1 tablespoon for drizzling

150 g/1 stick plus 2 tablespoons unsalted butter, softened

100 g/½ cup caster/white sugar

3 eggs, beaten

150 g/1 cup plus 2½ tablespoons self-raising flour

a pinch of salt

1 teaspoon baking powder

FOR THE BUTTERCREAM FILLING

100 g/6½ tablespoons unsalted butter, softened

150 g/1¼ cups icing/confectioners' sugar

1–2 drops vanilla extract

FOR THE TOPPING

1 tablespoon vodka

1 tablespoon Kahlúha

2 tablespoons instant coffee granules

250 g/2 cups plus 2 tablespoons icing/confectioner's sugar

a little warm water, if needed

30 g/1 oz. white chocolate

2 x 18-cm/7-inch shallow cake pans, lined and greased

SERVES 8–10

BOOZE RATING

If you can't find me at the bakery or the speakeasy, the next place to look is Joe's Coffee House. Ahhh, me and my friend Java. The hours and secrets we've shared. So this recipe, inspired by the wonder that is the White Russian, is in honour of the great bean.

Preheat the oven to 180°C (350°F) Gas 4.

Dissolve the coffee granules in a cup with the boiling water, vodka and Kahlúha.

In a mixing bowl, cream together the butter and sugar until light and fluffy. Add the beaten egg, a little at a time, folding through thoroughly between each addition. Sift the flour, salt and baking powder onto the mixture and, thoroughly but gently, fold all the ingredients together. Finally, add the coffee mixture to the bowl and give it a few more gentle stirs.

Divide the mixture between the prepared cake pans and bake in the preheated oven for about 25 minutes, until a skewer inserted into the middle of the cakes comes out clean.

Remove the cakes from the oven and prick them all over with a skewer. Drizzle ½ tablespoon vodka and ½ tablespoon Kahlúha over each cake, then allow them to cool completely on a wire rack.

To make the buttercream filling, cream together the butter, icing/confectioners' sugar and vanilla extract until smooth, then use to sandwich the cakes together.

For the topping, gently warm the vodka and Kahlúha, add the coffee granules and stir until dissolved. Add the liquid to the icing/confectioners' sugar, a little at a time, until you have a spreadable paste, adding a little warm water if the mixture is too dry. Ice the cake with the coffee icing, then leave somewhere cool to set.

Melt the white chocolate in a heatproof bowl set over a pan of simmering water and use a fork to drizzle it over the cake in a zigzag motion. Again, leave in a cool place to set and harden before serving.

PIMM'S O'CAKE

Now this cake and I have a very special relationship. This was the naughty little lemon drizzle that clamoured for my attention one night and whispered those three little words every girl wants to hear... 'Fancy a cocktail?' How could I resist? This is fabulous for afternoon tea or dinner or lunch... hell, I've had it for breakfast!

225 g/2 sticks unsalted butter
200 g/1 cup caster/white sugar
4 eggs, beaten
225 g/1¾ cups self-raising flour
finely grated zest and freshly squeezed juice of 1 orange
finely grated zest and freshly squeezed juice of 1 lemon
a handful of fresh mint, finely chopped
and of course... 150 ml/⅔ cup Pimm's

TO DECORATE
100 g/1 cup strawberries, sliced
a few fresh mint sprigs

a 450 g/1 lb. loaf pan, greased

SERVES 8–10

BOOZE RATING

Get that oven ready: preheat it to 180°C (350°F) Gas 4.

In a mixing bowl, cream together the butter and sugar until light and fluffy. Add the beaten egg, a little at a time, folding through thoroughly between each addition.

Sift the flour over the mixture and gently stir to a smooth consistency, then stir in the orange and lemon zest and the chopped mint. Add 50 ml/3½ tablespoons of the Pimm's, stir in gently, then pour the mixture into the prepared loaf pan. Pop in the preheated oven to bake for about 40–50 minutes.

Whilst you're waiting for the cake to bake, take the juice of your orange and lemon and stir it into the remaining Pimm's.

Once your cake is baked (you can check by inserting a skewer into the middle of the cake – if it comes out clean, then so are you), run a knife around the edge of the pan to loosen it, then turn it out onto a wire rack. Using a skewer, prick all over the top of the cake, then slowly and very carefully pour the Pimm's and juice mixture over the cake. You will need to allow the liquid to slowly absorb, so have patience and add a little at a time, then leave the cake to cool completely. Once cool, decorate the cake with strawberry slices and sprigs of mint.

Just a thought This little delight should be eaten at once if decorated, but if you can resist adding the strawberries, then it will keep in an airtight container for 3 days or so. It freezes beautifully, too.

PORT, CHOCOLATE & BLUEBERRY HEAVEN

This cake is a real showstopper. One to save for that hot date with the Mayor. He's sure to pardon your rap sheet after this little slice o' heaven! And which ones of yous out there knows why it's called a RAP sheet? Any ideas? Record of Arrest and Prosecution. How do I know? That's not a question to ask a lady!

200 g/1⅓ cups dried blueberries

150 ml/⅔ cup port

200 g/2 cups fresh blueberries

225 g/2 sticks unsalted butter, softened

200 g/1 cup caster/white sugar

3 large eggs, beaten

200 g/1⅔ cups self-raising flour

50 g/6 tablespoons unsweetened cocoa powder

150 g/5½ oz. dark/bittersweet chocolate, roughly chopped

6 small dariole moulds or individual pudding basins, greased

MAKES 6

BOOZE RATING

Put the dried blueberries in a bowl with 100 ml/7 tablespoons of the port and soak for at least 4 hours. Put the fresh blueberries in a separate bowl with the remaining port and soak for at least 2 hours.

Preheat the oven to 180°C (350°F) Gas 4.

In a mixing bowl, cream together the butter and sugar until light and fluffy. Add the beaten egg, a little at a time, folding through thoroughly between each addition.

Sift the flour and cocoa powder over the mixture and gently stir to a smooth consistency. Add the chocolate and the soaked dried blueberries, along with any unabsorbed soaking port and give it a final stir until well combined.

Drain the fresh blueberries and keep the port to one side (no sneaking a tipple!). Arrange the fresh blueberries in the bottom of the greased dariole moulds, dividing them equally between the moulds, then spoon over the cake batter and smooth level. Bake in the preheated oven for about 40–50 minutes, until a skewer inserted into the middle of the cakes comes out clean.

Turn the cakes out onto serving plates, fruit side up, then take the port that you saved from the fresh blueberries and slowly drizzle it over the top of the cakes. Allow to cool and serve with a big, smug grin.

TEA BREAD, LONG ISLAND STYLE

2 teaspoons gin

2 teaspoons vodka

2 teaspoons rum

2 teaspoons tequila

2 teaspoons triple sec

150 g/¾ cup caster/white sugar

50 g/⅓ cup sultanas/golden raisins

50 g/⅓ cup glacé/candied cherries, roughly chopped

100 g/6½ tablespoons unsalted butter, softened

1 teaspoon bicarbonate of soda/baking soda

1 egg, beaten

1 teaspoon baking powder

175 g/1⅓ cups plus 1 tablespoon plain/all-purpose flour

FOR DRIZZLING

1 tablespoon gin

1 tablespoon vodka

1 tablespoon rum

1 tablespoon tequila

1 tablespoon triple sec

a 450 g/1 lb. loaf pan, lined and greased

SERVES 8–10

BOOZE RATING

Bread, the staff of life, or in this case, the dapper walking stick to fight them off with at the brightest gin palace in town. I love gorging on this heavenly stuff on a chilly winter's evening and for once, I actually do wash it down with a cup of tea. Real tea. Don't worry, I won't let it become a habit.

Preheat the oven to 180°C (350°F) Gas 4.

Take a large, heavy saucepan – the kind you usually save for hitting wannabe burglars – and add all the lovely hooch to it along with 70 ml/5 tablespoons water, and the sugar, sultanas/golden raisins, cherries, butter and bicarbonate of soda/baking soda. Set the pan over a medium heat and gradually bring to the boil, then keep it at a rolling boil for 10 minutes whilst gently stirring.

Remove the mixture from the heat and put to one side to cool for about 5 minutes, then add the beaten egg and the baking powder to the pan with the fruit mixture and stir in. Sift the flour over the mixture and give everything a good stir, then spoon into the prepared loaf pan. Bake in the preheated oven for 40–50 minutes, until a skewer inserted into the middle of the cake comes out clean. Remove from the oven and prick the cake all over with a skewer.

Mix the 'drizzling' hooch together in a jug/pitcher and slowly pour over the cake. Allow the cake to cool for 5–10 minutes, then remove from the pan. Remove the paper and let it cool for a further 20–30 minutes on a wire rack.

Just a thought Once you've mastered this tease of a take on tea bread, it's a great variation on the bread and butter pudding recipe. You can use any one of the hooches or a combination instead of the suggested amaretto. Wrapped in kitchen foil, this bread keeps really well and, just like me, gets even better with age.

THE BEE'S KNEES

Now flappers, you know what they say for colds: honey and lemon. Well, then this cake has the power to see off any cough, sniffle or croak because it's just that... with perhaps just a hint of gin sneaked in there. I mean really, what's a cake without gin? Hell, what's life without gin? Gin and I have a long and loving relationship, although I must admit to not always being faithful. For this recipe, I think Hendrick's works best as it's a highly aromatic tipple.

225 g/2 sticks unsalted butter, softened

250 g/1 cup clear, runny honey

100 g/½ cup dark muscovado sugar

250 g/2 cups self-raising flour

3 large eggs

50 ml/3½ tablespoons gin (such as Hendrick's)

FOR THE TOPPING
200 g/1⅔ cups icing/confectioners' sugar

grated zest of 1 lemon

a 20-cm/8-inch loose-based cake pan, greased

SERVES 10–12

BOOZE RATING

Preheat the oven to 160°C (325°F) Gas 3.

Put the butter, honey and sugar in a saucepan set over a gentle heat and melt slowly. Bring to the boil for a minute, then remove from the heat and set aside to cool for about 15 minutes.

Sift the flour into a large mixing bowl and beat in the eggs. Add the honey mixture and stir in, then add the gin and keep stirring. Don't worry if it looks a little runny – just so long as it's smooth.

Pour the mixture into the prepared cake pan and bake in the preheated oven for 50–60 minutes. As always flappers, do the skewer test; if it comes out clean, then you're home dry. If not, give the cake a little more love in the oven, but you may want to lay a sheet of kitchen foil over the top of the cake to stop it from getting too much of a tan! When cooked through, remove from the oven and turn out onto a wire rack to cool completely.

To make the topping, add a few drops of water to the icing/confectioners' sugar and mix to a spreadable consistency. Spoon the icing over the cake, decorate with a sprinkling of lemon zest and leave to set. Call your honey and let the cake work its magic.

OLD FASHIONED, REFASHIONED

100 g/⅔ cup glacé/candied cherries, roughly chopped

100 ml/6½ tablespoons bourbon whiskey

50 ml/3½ tablespoons freshly squeezed orange juice

225 g/2 sticks unsalted butter, softened

150 g/¾ cup golden caster/natural cane sugar

3 large eggs, beaten

225 g/1¾ cups self-raising flour

a pinch of ground nutmeg

soft brown sugar, to decorate

FOR THE FILLING

2 oranges, peeled, segmented and roughly chopped

50 ml/3½ tablespoons bourbon whiskey

85 g/5½ tablespoons unsalted butter, softened

175 g/1½ cups icing/confectioners' sugar, plus extra for dusting

a splash of vanilla extract

orange zest, to decorate (optional)

a deep 20-cm/8-inch springform cake pan, greased

SERVES 10–12

BOOZE RATING

An Old Fashioned for me is always made with a great bourbon, so splash out on a real doozey from a quality bootlegger and stay clear of those amateurs and their homemade vats of firewater! Ma O'Reilley is still pencilling in her eyebrows after her little homebrew explosion.

Put the cherries in a bowl with the 100 ml/¼ cup bourbon and the orange juice and allow to stand for at least 1 hour. Preheat the oven to 180°C (350°F) Gas 4.

In a large mixing bowl, cream together the butter and sugar until light and fluffy, then add the eggs, one at a time, and mix in. Sift the flour and ground nutmeg over the mixture and fold in thoroughly. Strain the cherries (reserving the soaking liquid), add them to your cake batter and stir in. Pour the batter into the prepared cake pan and bake in the preheated oven for 40–50 minutes (you may want to put a sheet of kitchen foil over the top of the cake towards the end of the baking time to stop the top getting too dark).

While the cake is cooking, let the orange segments for the filling have a good old paddle about in the 50 ml/3½ tablespooons bourbon for at least 30 minutes.

When the cake is baked, allow to cool for 5 minutes, then turn out onto a wire rack. Whilst still warm, prick the cake all over with a skewer and gently pour over half of the reserved cherry-soaking liquid, then leave to cool completely. Once cool, take a very sharp knife and split the cake in two, horizontally. Prick the cut cake surfaces and gently smear over the remaining cherry-soaking liquid.

In a large mixing bowl, whisk together the butter and icing/confectioner's sugar until creamy and light. Add a splash of vanilla extract and stir in. Smear half of the buttercream filling on each cut surface of the cake. Strain the oranges and arrange them over the buttercream on the base cake, then gently sandwich the two sides together, but don't press down too hard – a little love goes a long way! If you're feeling particularly frisky, decorate the top of your cake with pared orange zest and a sprinkling of confectioners'/icing sugar.

LIMBO FRUIT CAKE

50 g/⅓ cup dried mango chunks

50 g/⅓ cup dried papaya chunks

100 ml/6½ tablespoons dark rum

100 ml/6½ tablespoons port or red wine

100 g/½ cup chopped canned or fresh pineapple

100 g/⅔ cup glacé/candied cherries, chopped

250 g/2¼ sticks unsalted butter, softened

200 g/1 cup caster/white sugar

4 large eggs

250 g/2 cups self-raising flour

2 teaspoons ground cinnamon

2 teaspoons ground ginger

100 g/generous 1 cup desiccated/shredded coconut

2 tablespoons soft brown sugar

FOR THE TOPPING

dried fruit and nuts of your choice, jam (to glaze), or rolled fondant icing

a 23-cm/9-inch ring cake pan, greased and double-lined with baking parchment

SERVES 10–12

BOOZE RATING

Ahhh, my glorious Limbo Fruit Cake – so called because after a particularly generous helping, Officer O'Malley and I... well, our relationship reached new depths. If you're thinking of serving this for Christmas tea, be prepared for some festive antics as it packs a rum punch and a half – you have been warned. Ideally, soak your fruit for a month or two beforehand.

1–2 months ahead of baking, put the dried mango and papaya in a bowl and add the dark rum and port, cover with clingfilm/plastic wrap and leave in the fridge to soak until you are ready to make the cake. About an hour before making the cake, add the chopped pineapple and cherries to the soaking fruit, stir and set aside.

Preheat the oven to 180°C (350°F) Gas 4.

In a separate mixing bowl, cream together the butter and sugar until light and fluffy, then add the eggs, one at a time, and mix in. Sift the flour and spices over the mixture and gently stir to a smooth consistency, then stir in the coconut. Strain the soaked fruit and add to the mixture, reserving any soaking liquid.

Spoon the mixture into the prepared cake pan and sprinkle with soft brown sugar. Bake in the preheated oven for 60 minutes, then test to see whether the middle is cooked by inserting a skewer. If it's not quite cooked, give it another 5–10 minutes, then test again.

Once cooked through, turn the cake out onto a large plate and prick all over with a skewer. Pour the reserved soaking liquor slowly over the cake so that the cake is saturated, then allow to cool. Decorate if you wish (see below) and serve.

Just a thought This cake is a joy to decorate so let your imagination go wild. Add extra fruit or caramelized nuts to the top and wrap with a bright ribbon, or cover the cake with jam, then fondant icing. This cake will keep for a while in an air-tight container, so you've plenty of time to think about how you'd like to decorate it.

MINT JULEP CREAMS

Whilst making these little beauties is kids play, the real adult fun is in the decoration and design... And, of course, the powerful alcoholic kick! Have these as your after dinner mint and I guarantee that the guests will be high-kicking and low tale telling in no time.

400 g/3⅓ cups icing/
confectioners' sugar, plus
a little extra for dusting

2 teaspoons double/heavy cream

1 egg white

2 teaspoons crème de menthe

1–2 drops green food colouring

2 teaspoons Bourbon whiskey
(the paler in colour the better)

1–2 drops peppermint extract

TO DECORATE

50 g/2 oz. plain chocolate

50 g/2 oz. milk chocolate

50 g/2 oz. white chocolate

about 30 small fresh mint leaves

MAKES ABOUT 30

BOOZE RATING

Put all the ingredients in a large mixing bowl and mix to a stiff paste that can be rolled and shaped. (If it is too sticky, add some more icing/confectioners' sugar)

Lightly dust a work surface with icing/confectioners' sugar and roll the paste into a sausage shape (about 4 cm/1½ inches across). Cut off slices about 1 cm/½ inch thick. Place the slices onto a sheet of non-stick baking parchment and leave to dry.

Once the creams are dry, melt the plain chocolate in a heatproof bowl set over a pan of simmering water. Divide the mint slices into 3 portions and dip one third of them into the melted plain chocolate, to cover half of the slice. Whilst the chocolate is still wet, press a mint leaf into the chocolate, lay the slice back onto the baking parchment and leave to set. Repeat, dipping the next portion into the melted milk chocolate, and the final third of the slices into the white chocolate, and leave them all to set. Alternatively, carefully dip a mint leaf into one of the melted chocolates, place on top of the Julep cream and leave to set.

Just a thought These will need to be stored in an airtight container but will keep for… well I'm going to guess at 2–3 days. They've never made it past 2–3 hours at my place.

small measures

FLUTTERING GREEN FAIRY CAKES

'Why Officer – these little fancies? They're just your childhood fairy cakes like Grandma used to make. Nothing of interest here. Officer...' These beauties may not make you popular with the law, but I guarantee you'll be guest number 1 if you take a batch of these to your next shindig.

200 g/1¾ sticks unsalted butter, softened
150 g/¾ cup caster/white sugar
3 large eggs, beaten
200 g/1⅔ cups self-raising flour
2–3 drops of vanilla extract
100 ml/6½ tablespoons absinthe

FOR THE BUTTERCREAM FILLING
100 g/6½ tablespoons unsalted butter, softened
200 g/1 cup icing/confectioners' sugar, plus extra for dusting
2–3 drops green food colouring
1 tablespoon absinthe

a 12-hole cake pan lined with the darned cutest cupcake cases you can find!
2 piping bags fitted with large star nozzles/tips

MAKES 12

BOOZE RATING

Preheat the oven to 180°C (350°F) Gas 4.

In a mixing bowl, cream together the butter and sugar until light and fluffy. Add the beaten egg, a little at a time, folding through thoroughly between each addition.

Sift the flour into the bowl and gently stir to a smooth consistency, then add the vanilla extract and half the absinthe and fold in well. Spoon the cake batter into the cases so that each case is about two thirds full and bake in the preheated oven for about 15 minutes, until golden brown.

Whilst still warm, prick each cake a couple of times with a skewer. Very slowly drizzle a little more absinthe over the top of each cake until you have used all the remaining absinthe, then allow to cool.

Once cool, cut the domed top off each cake so that you have circles of cake approximately 3–4 cm/1½ inches in diameter, then cut each circle in half and set aside. Repeat for all the cakes.

For the buttercream filling, cream together the butter, icing/confectioners' sugar and absinthe. If the mixture is too wet, add a little more icing/confectioners' sugar. Divide the buttercream between two bowls and colour one half with the green food colouring. Spoon the buttercream into the piping bags and pipe a swirl on top of each cake so that half are plain and half are green. Finally, pop two semicircles of the reserved cake onto the top of each fairy cake to create the 'wings', and dust with a little more icing/confectioners' sugar to serve.

KIKI'S STICKACULAR KIRSCH POPS

What's not to love? It's chocolate, it's cherries, it's kirsch, it's on a STICK! This is the absolute perfect treat for the most adult of birthday parties. So next time the barman asks you whether you want it straight up or on the rocks, say it loud and say it proud, folks: 'Make mine on a stick!'

225 g/2 sticks unsalted butter, softened

200 g/1 cup golden caster/ natural cane sugar

4 eggs

200 g/1⅔ cups self-raising flour

50 g/6 tablespoons unsweetened cocoa powder

100 ml/6½ tablespoons Kirsch

300 g/10½ oz. canned cherries, drained and finely chopped

200 g/7 oz. white chocolate

400 g/14 oz. dark/bittersweet chocolate

sugar sprinkles, to decorate

a 20-cm/8-inch round cake pan, greased

a baking sheet lined with non-stick baking parchment

25–30 lollipop/popsicle sticks

styrofoam, or something similar to stick the pops in whilst they are setting

MAKES 25–30 CAKE POPS

BOOZE RATING

Preheat the oven to 180°C (350°F) Gas 4.

In a large mixing bowl, cream together the butter and the sugar. Break in the eggs, one by one, stirring between each addition. Sift the flour and cocoa powder over the mix and gently stir to a smooth consistency, then add half of the Kirsch and the chopped cherries and stir in.

Pour the batter into the prepared cake pan and pop in the preheated oven for 40–50 minutes, until a skewer inserted into the middle of the cakes comes out clean. Turn the cake out onto a wire rack to cool completely.

Once cool, finely crumble the cake into a large heatproof mixing bowl and drizzle over the remaining Kirsch.

Melt the white chocolate in a heatproof bowl set over a pan of barely simmering water, then pour it into the bowl with the cake crumbs and stir to bring it all together. Take spoonfuls of the mixture and form into 25–30 small balls. Put the balls onto the prepared baking sheet and chill in the fridge for 20–30 minutes.

Once the balls are cool, remove them from the fridge and insert a lollipop/ popsicle stick about one third of the way into the ball.

Very gently melt the dark chocolate and, one at a time, dip the cake pops into the chocolate. Don't go crazy here, flappers! Just a straight down dip in and out so that the cake pop is completely covered – don't swirl it around in the chocolate or you may lose bits of cake, and that's a criminal activity if ever I heard of one! Very gently tap off any excess chocolate and, whilst still wet, sprinkle over the sugar sprinkles. Put the lollipop stick in the styrofoam to stand and set for about 20–30 minutes, then put your hair in bunches and lick on the best lolly in town!

BRAMBLE BROWNIES

Stop right there! I can see you skipping past this recipe, shaking your head and thinking of your waistline, but it's OK DOKAY, these have fruit in! And as we all know, you can never get enough fruit, especially when it's fermented. With these you'll be able to convince anyone to do anything for you. Use your powers wisely, young flappers!

50 g/½ cup blackberries
50 g/½ cup raspberries
125 ml/½ cup crème de mure
185 g/1½ sticks unsalted butter, softened
185 g/6½ oz. dark/bittersweet chocolate (as with all the good things in life, you're looking for at least 70% proof on the chocolate)
3 large eggs
225 g/1 cup plus 2 tablespoons golden caster/natural cane sugar
100 g/¾ cup plain/all-purpose flour
50 g/6 tablespoons unsweetened cocoa powder
a tonne of willpower

a 20 x 20-cm/8 x 8-inch brownie pan, greased

MAKES 16
(technically speaking, but if all the mix makes it into the cake pan, well then you're a better woman than me.)

BOOZE RATING

Wash and drain the berries, then put them in a bowl with 100 ml/7 tablespoons of the crème de mure and leave for at least an hour at room temperature.

Preheat the oven to 180°C (350°F) Gas 4.

Very gently, melt the butter and chocolate in a heatproof bowl set over a pan of barely simmering water, then leave to cool.

In a large mixing bowl, whisk together the eggs and sugar until creamy, frothy and light as a feather. Gently fold the chocolate and butter mixture into the egg mixture. You don't want to beat out all the air here, so gently does it, sweetcheeks. Sift the flour and cocoa powder over the mix and again, gently, gently fold. Add the mixed fruit and any remaining liquor that hasn't been absorbed by the fruit. Again, just a few gentle folding stirs here. Like all things in life, keep them wanting more, so hold back and don't stir away like a crazy woman.

Spoon the mixture into your brownie pan and slide it into the preheated oven to bake for about 20 minutes. If after 20 minutes the middle of the brownie is still wobbly, put it back in for a further 5–10 minutes. Remove the brownie from the oven and turn it out onto a wire rack and – and this is where the willpower comes in – allow to cool.

Once cool, cut into quarters, then quarters again, and serve.

Just a thought So what about the remaining crème de mure I hear you cry? That's your reward for not eating all of these before they've even made it to the cooling rack. Add to a champagne flute and top up with the bubbles of your choice, then sit back and marvel at how wonderful you are!

FLAPPERTASTIC FRAISES DES BOIS COOKIES

Fraises des bois – sounds like a dancehall dame I used to know, but hold that thought and add a little Kikification and you get to crème de fraises des bois: strawberry liquor. I know! Two of life's finest ingredients, strawberries and liquor. You just know that these are going to be a knock out! Perfect for an elegant picnic... or for nibbling on the subway. A working girl has gotta do, what a working girl has gotta do!

200 g/1⅓ cups dried strawberries

25 ml/2 tablespoons crème de fraises des bois

25 ml/2 tablespoons strawberry vodka

125 g/1 stick unsalted butter, softened

125 g/⅔ cup golden caster/natural cane sugar

1 egg, beaten

125 g/1 cup plain/all-purpose flour

1 teaspoon baking powder

a baking sheet, well greased

MAKES 12–14

BOOZE RATING

Soak the dried strawberries in the crème de fraises des bois and vodka for at least 5 hours, or ideally overnight, to rehydrate.

Preheat the oven to 190°C (375°F) Gas 5.

In a large mixing bowl, cream together the butter and sugar until light and fluffy. Add the beaten egg, soaked strawberries (plus any remaining soaking liquor), flour and baking powder and stir well.

With a tablespoon, spoon dollops of the mixture onto the prepared baking sheet, spaced well apart. Bake the cookies in the preheated oven for 12–15 minutes until golden brown.

Just a thought These are delicious served warm from the oven with a blob of ice cream… strawberry flavour of course!

24 CARAT CAKES

Diamonds may be a girl's best friend, but a little gold goes a long way in my book. Thanks to those fabulous people at Goldschläger – who add gold leaf to their cinnamon schnapps – you have, you heard me folks, genuine, honest to goodness, 24 carat carrot cakes!

175 g/¾ cup soft brown sugar

250 g/2 cups plain/all-purpose flour

2 teaspoons baking powder

2 teaspoons ground cinnamon

3 eggs, beaten

225 ml/scant 1 cup light vegetable oil

2 teaspoons vanilla extract

175 g/6 oz. cooked carrots, mashed

125 g/1¼ cups chopped pecans

200 ml/¾ cup Goldschläger

1 small raw carrot

FOR THE CREAM CHEESE FROSTING

200 g/¾ cup soft cream cheese

100 g/¾ cup icing/confectioners' sugar

2 tablespoons sour cream

a 20-cm/8-inch square baking pan, 5-cm/2-inches deep, greased and lined with non-stick baking parchment

MAKES 12

BOOZE RATING

Preheat the oven to 180°C (350°F) Gas 4.

Put the sugar in a large mixing bowl and sift in the flour, baking powder and cinnamon. Add the beaten eggs, oil and vanilla extract and mix together well. Add the cooked mashed carrots and pecans to the bowl and mix again. Finally, add half of the Goldschläger and fold through until everything is well combined.

Pour the cake batter into the prepared baking pan and ensure that it is evenly spread into the corners – give the pan a little shake and shimmy and it should help the mixture to spread evenly. Put the pan in the preheated oven and bake for 45–55 minutes.

While the cake is cooking, finely grate the raw carrot into a small bowl, then pour over 50 ml/¼ cup of the Goldschläger and set it to one side.

Use a skewer inserted into the middle of the cake to make sure it is cooked – if it comes out clean, then you're home and dry, if not, put it back in for a further 5 minutes. Remove from the oven and allow to cool for a few minutes, then turn the cake out onto a plate and gently pull away the baking parchment.

With a skewer, prick all over the still warm cake. Slowly pour over the remaining Goldschläger so that it gradually seeps into the cake but leaves some of the gold leaf on the surface and the cake shines like the top of the Chrysler Building!

To make the cream cheese frosting, just whisk all the ingredients together and you're good to go! Cut the cake into bite-sized pieces and spoon a dollop of cream cheese frosting onto each piece, finishing with a sprinkle of your Goldschläger-soaked raw carrot.

MARVELLOUS MIXOLOGY MANDARIN MUFFINS

200 g/1¾ sticks unsalted butter, softened

150 g/¾ cup caster/white sugar

3 large eggs

200 g/ self-raising flour

a 410-g/14-oz. can mandarin oranges (drained, but hold on to that juice)

3 tablespoons whiskey, plus 2 tablespoons to drizzle

FOR THE TOPPINGS
Go crazy!

100 g/3½ oz. dark chocolate

100 g/3½ oz. milk chocolate

100 g/3½ oz. white chocolate

mandarin slices

grated zest of 1 orange

or if you're feeling particularly devilish and let's face it, who isn't, make a little chocolate glaze but use a splash of whiskey rather than water:

200 g/1⅓ cups icing/confectioners' sugar

30 g/2 tablespoons unsweetened cocoa powder

a splash of whiskey

a 6-hole muffin pan, lined with muffin cases or liners

MAKES 6 LARGE MUFFINS

BOOZE RATING

Who doesn't love a cute little muffin? I know I do. Part of the fun of these little fellas is playing with the decoration. As always, feel free to add your own marvellous mixology to these muffins. Have you thought about adding cocoa powder to the flour? What about adding chocolate chips? You know you could ice with dark, milk or white chocolate? How about a healthy topping of orange water buttercream frosting? Oh, the endless possibilities!

Preheat the oven to 180°C (350°F) Gas 4.

In a large mixing bowl, cream together the butter and sugar. Break in the eggs, one by one, and beat in. Sift the flour over the mixture and gently stir to a smooth consistency, then add the mandarins and whiskey and stir again so that the mandarin segments begin to break up in the mix. Spoon the batter into the muffin cases (to about two thirds full) and bake in the preheated oven for about 15–20 minutes, until golden on top.

Remove the cakes from the oven and prick each cake a couple of times with a skewer. Combine the drizzling whiskey with a splash of the mandarin juice and drizzle a little over each cake, then allow them to cool.

Decorate the cakes with the melted chocolate along with a mandarin slice or two and some orange zest.

Just a thought I like to split the mix and make half plain and half chocolate. To make the chocolate versions just substitute 50 g/generous ⅓ cup of the flour for unsweetened cocoa powder and add a handful of chocolate chips. Genius!

tipsy tarts

NEW YORK SOUR PEAR TARTS

Ahh New York, what a town. I could tell you some stories about hazy days and even shadier nights spent there, but that'd be a whole different kind of book. A New York Sour is a classic cocktail and while New York is better known as the Big Apple, trust me, for this recipe, it's pears all the way.

1 pack ready-made sweet shortcrust pastry

FOR THE POACHED PEARS
300 ml/1¼ cups red wine

200 ml/¾ cup whiskey

200 g/1 cup caster/white sugar

grated zest and freshly squeezed juice of 1 unwaxed lemon

2 teaspoons vanilla extract

2 large ripe pears, peeled but with the stalk intact

FOR THE CRÈME PATISSIÈRE
300 ml/1¼ cups semi-skimmed milk

2 teaspoons vanilla extract

25 g/3 tablespoons plain/all-purpose flour

2 eggs

50 g/¼ cup caster/white sugar

a 14-cm/5½-inch pastry cutter
4 loose-bottomed 12-cm/5-inch, individual tartlet pans, greased

MAKES 4 TARTS

BOOZE RATING

Preheat the oven to 190°C (375°F) Gas 5.

On a floured surface, roll out the pastry to 5 mm/¼ inch thick. Use the pastry cutter to cut out 4 rounds. Line the tart pans with the rounds, prick the bottom of each pastry case, line with baking parchment and fill with baking beans. Bake the cases for about 15 minutes, until golden, then set on a wire rack and let cool.

It's time for those pears to go for a dip! Put the wine, whiskey, sugar, lemon zest and juice and vanilla in a large saucepan and warm gently. Add the pears, ensuring that they are fully submerged, cover the pan and let poach for 20–30 minutes until tender all the way through. Remove the pears from the pan but hold on to that liquor! Set the pears to one side to cool on a plate.

Now for the gooey gorgeousness of crème patissière. Put the milk and vanilla in a pan and heat until almost boiling. In a heatproof bowl, beat together the flour, eggs and sugar to create a smooth paste. Slowly (and carefully!) add half of the hot vanilla milk, stirring all the while. Pour this mixture back into the milk pan and keep stirring! Cook the crème patissière over a gentle heat for a few more minutes until thickened, then set aside and allow to cool.

To assemble the tarts, spoon the crème patissière into each tart case to about one third full. Core the poached pears and cut each one in half. From the bottom of the pear, cut long incisions (as if slicing thinly) but stop two-thirds of the way up so the slices are still joined at the top. Place a pear half in each of the cases, gently 'fanning' out the bottom of the pear.

Quickly boil the remaining red wine and whiskey poaching liquid, reducing it down until it turns syrupy. Spoon a couple of teaspoons of this syrup over each pear and serve immediately.

GUILTY GUINNESS MINCE PIES

250 g/9 oz. mincemeat

100 ml/⅔ cup Guinness

350 g/2¾ cups plain/
all-purpose flour

a pinch of salt

225 g/2 sticks unsalted butter,
chilled and cubed

1 egg

about 100 ml/6½ tablespoons
ice cold water

a 12-hole tart pan

*an 8-cm/3¼-inch round pastry
cutter*

*a round pastry cutter, slightly
bigger than the holes in your
tart pan*

*a small christmas tree pastry
cutter (optional)*

MAKES 12

BOOZE RATING

A nod to our Irish cousins here and their magical elixir of Guinness. I know that we all go crazy for St Patrick's day in March, but for me, one day a year is not enough of a celebration so I like bring a little Irish stout into Christmas preparations, too. It's best to allow the mincemeat and the Guinness to get to know each other for a few hours at least beforehand.

Put the mincemeat and Guinness into a large bowl, stir and leave to stand for a few hours.

To make the pastry, sift the flour and salt into a large mixing bowl. Add the butter and gently rub the mixture between your fingers until the texture is like fine breadcrumbs. Add the egg and stir in, then slowly add, drop by drop (you may not need it all), enough of the cold water to make a stiff dough. Bring the dough together with your fingers and then wrap in clingfilm/plastic wrap and let it rest in the fridge for about 30 minutes.

Preheat the oven to 200°C (400°F) Gas 6.

Dust your work surface with flour and take the pastry dough from the fridge. Roll out about two thirds of the pastry to around 3–4 mm/⅛ inch thick. Stamp out pastry rounds with the cutter and use them to line the holes of your tart pan. Fill each pastry case two-thirds full with the mincemeat and Guinness mixture.

Roll out the remaining pastry to the same thickness and cut out slightly smaller circles for the pie lids. If you wish, you can cut small christmas trees out of the lids to decorate, but if you are worried about all that gorgeous Guinness making a bid for freedom, just a small slit in the lid to let out the steam will suffice. Very lightly dampen the edges of the base with a little cold water and press the lids on to your bases. Bake in the preheated oven for 12–15 minutes until golden brown.

TARTE 'TUT TUT'!

The neighbours are always wagging their fingers and tutting their tongues at my shenanigans, so I thought I'd really give them something to shout about and Kikify a classic Tarte Tatin. I can just hear those prohibition purists crying out, 'Mon dieu! This dame has no shame!' On that note, let's go the whole kit and caboodle and plump for ready-made pastry. Life is too short and just think of all that time you could spend swinging the night away with someone dreamy, instead!

6 apples (I like to use the pink-skinned ones, but any good quality, not bitter apple is fine)

50 g/3 tablespoons unsalted butter

50 g/¼ cup packed soft brown sugar

100 ml/6½ tablespoons Calvados

1 x 270-g/9½-oz. pack ready-made filo/phyllo pastry – trust me on this!

FOR THE TOPPING

200 ml/¾ cup crème fraîche

1 tablespoon Calvados

1 tablespoon icing/confectioners' sugar

a large baking sheet, greased

SERVES 6–8

BOOZE RATING

Peel the apples and cut them into quarters. Remove the cores and slice each quarter into 4 pieces.

Take a heavy bottomed frying pan and melt the butter and brown sugar over a very gentle heat until the sugar starts to caramelize. Add the apple slices and coat in the butter and sugar, then pour in the Calvados. Turn down the heat to low and allow the apples to cook for about 10 minutes, until they are beginning to soften. Take off the heat and set aside to cool. When cooled, drain most of the liquid from the apple mixture (reserve this to use later).

Preheat the oven to 190°C (375°F) Gas 5.

For the tarts, you need your pastry to be about 4 sheets of filo/phyllo thick, so remove the pastry from the packet and peel apart as necessary. Cut each set of sheets into squares measuring about 8–10 cm/4–5 inches. Take a filo/phyllo square and spoon 1 tablespoon of the apple mixture into the middle. Pull up the 4 corners and twist them so that you have a small parcel. Brush the parcel with a little of the liquor reserved from draining the apples, then place on the prepared baking sheet. Repeat until you have used all your pastry and apple mixture.

Bake the tarts in the preheated oven for approximately 15 minutes, or until the pastry is lightly golden brown and cooked through.

While the tarts are baking, make the topping. Put the crème fraîche in a bowl with the Calvados and icing/confectioners' sugar and mix together well.

Serve the tarts immediately with a generous helping of the topping. Hey presto!

LIMONCELLO TARTLETS

FOR THE SWEET PASTRY TART CASES

225 g/1¾ cups plain/all-purpose flour, plus extra for dusting

100 g/6½ tablespoons unsalted butter, chilled and cubed

80 g/scant ½ cup caster/white sugar

grated zest of 1 lemon

a handful of fresh mint leaves, finely chopped

1 large egg

2–3 tablespoons milk

grated zest of 1 lemon

200 g/7 oz. of the best white chocolate you can find

FOR THE FILLING

100 ml/6½ tablespoons limoncello

300 g/10½ oz. lemon curd

250 g/9 oz. cream cheese

200 g/1⅔ cups icing/confectioners' sugar

100 ml/6½ tablespoons double/heavy cream

grated zest of 2 lemons

a 12-hole tart pan, greased

an 8-cm/3½-inch round pastry cutter

MAKES 12

BOOZE RATING

A few years ago, I spent a blissful summer dancing my way along the Amalfi coast with the bright and beautiful things. We spent many a happy early hour sipping ice cold limoncello to soothe our fevered brows. This is a good ol' U S of A nod and a wink to that wondrous yellow elixir, with just a hint of dreamy white chocolate to up the ante.

Put the flour and cubed butter in a mixing bowl and gently rub them between your fingers until the texture resembles fine breadcrumbs, then mix in the sugar, lemon zest and chopped mint. Add the egg and stir in, then add enough milk to bring it all together to form a soft dough. Wrap the pastry dough in clingfilm/plastic wrap and let it rest in the fridge for about 20–30 minutes. Meanwhile, preheat the oven to 190°C (375°F) Gas 5.

Remove the pastry from the fridge and, on a lightly floured surface, roll it out to 5 mm/¼ inch thick. Use the pastry cutter to cut out rounds, rerolling any leftover pastry, until you have 12 rounds, then use them to line the holes of the baking pan. Prick the bottom of each pastry case, line with a small square of baking parchment, fill with baking beans and bake blind in the preheated oven for about 15 minutes. Remove each case from the baking pan and set on a wire rack to cool.

In a heatproof bowl set over a pan of barely simmering water, gently melt 150 g/5½ oz. of the chocolate and allow to cool to a spreadable consistency. Spread a thin layer over the bottom of each pastry case, then pop the cases in an airtight container and put in the fridge for 20 minutes to set the chocolate.

For the filling, stir the limoncello into the lemon curd. In a separate bowl, combine the cream cheese, icing/confectioners' sugar, cream and lemon zest.

Take the tart cases from the fridge and spoon 1 generous teaspoon of the lemon mixture into each one, followed by 1 generous teaspoon of the cream cheese mixture. Grate the remaining chocolate and sprinkle over the top of each tart. Return to the airtight container and chill for a further 30 minutes before serving.

KISS & TELL TART

1 pack ready-made shortcrust pastry
OR
225 g/1¾ cups plain/all-purpose flour (plus extra for dusting)
100 g/6½ tablespoons unsalted butter, chilled and cubed
½ teaspoon salt
about 100 ml/6½ tablespoons ice cold water

FOR THE FILLING
100 g/⅔ cup dried cranberries
125 ml/½ cup vodka
125 ml/½ cup amaretto
3 tablespoons orange jam or thin-shred marmalade
100 g/3½ oz. clementines, peeled and roughly chopped
100 g/¾ cup fresh cranberries
150 g/5½ oz. amaretto biscuits/cookies, crumbled

TO SERVE
vanilla ice cream
cinnamon, to dust

4 heart-shaped tart pans

SERVES 4

BOOZE RATING

Now folks, those buttoned down, starched knickered matrons may tell you that store-bought pasty is a crime in the kitchen but I figure, we're all going to jail if the cops find these recipes, so we may as well go for the full RAP sheet. But, if you do have the time and the inclination, I've jotted down an easy peasy pastry recipe for you.

Put the dried cranberries for the filling in a bowl, pour over 50 ml/3½ tablespoons of the vodka and 50 ml/3½ tablespoons of the amaretto and leave to rehydrate for at least 2 hours.

If you're making your own pastry, put the flour, butter and salt in a large mixing bowl and gently rub them between your fingers until the texture resembles fine breadcrumbs. Drop by drop, slowly add enough of the cold water to make a stiff dough then bring the dough together with your fingers. Wrap the pastry in clingfilm/plastic wrap and let it rest in the fridge for about 20–30 minutes.

Put 2 tablespoons of the orange jam in a saucepan with the remaining vodka and amaretto. Gently warm through so that the jam becomes runny. Add the clementines, fresh cranberries and the strained rehydrated cranberries. Simmer over a low heat and keep stirring for around 10 minutes, then set aside to cool.

Preheat the oven to 180°C (350°F) Gas 4. Remove the pastry from the fridge. On a lightly floured surface, roll it out to 5 mm/¼ inch thick and use it to line the tart pans. Prick the bottom of each pastry case, line with baking parchment and fill with baking beans. Bake the cases for about 15–20 minutes, then take them out of the oven and remove the baking parchment and baking beans. Spread a little of the remaining orange jam over the base of each pastry case. With a slotted spoon, fill the cases with the cooked fruit mixture, dividing it equally between the pans. Be careful not to add too much liquid. Sprinkle the crumbled amaretto biscuits/cookies over the top, then return to the oven for a final 5 minutes.

Serve the tarts with vanilla ice cream and dust with cinnamon.

SHIMMY SHERRY SHAKEWELL

FOR THE SWEET PASTRY TART CASE
125 g/1 cup plain/all-purpose flour, plus extra for dusting
75 g/5 tablespoons unsalted butter, chilled and cubed
25 g/2 tablespoons caster/white sugar
1 large egg
2–3 tablespoons milk (yes milk, not alcohol. I know, I was surprised too!)

FOR THE FILLING
1 tablespoon raspberry jam
75 ml/5 tablespoons Oloroso sherry
150 g/1 stick plus 2 tablespoons unsalted butter, softened
150 g/¾ cup caster/white sugar
3 eggs, beaten
175 g/1 cup ground almonds

TO DECORATE
a handful of fresh raspberries
flaked/slivered almonds

a 20 cm/8-inch fluted tart pan, well greased

SERVES 8–10

BOOZE RATING

The joy of sherry. No, don't make that face. We're not talking about the Christmas cream sherry that Grandma knocks back, but the joyful, wonderful world of sherry – everything from the palest Fino to the darkest, richest Oloroso. Heaven. So this cake honours sherry and its natural friend, the almond.

Put the flour and cubed butter in a mixing bowl and gently rub them between your fingers until the texture resembles fine breadcrumbs, then mix in the sugar. Add the egg and stir in, then add enough milk to bring it all together to form a soft dough. Wrap the pastry dough in clingfilm/plastic wrap and let it rest in the fridge for about 20–30 minutes. Meanwhile, preheat the oven to 180°C (350°F) Gas 4.

Remove the pastry from the fridge and, on a lightly floured surface, roll it out to 5 mm/¼ inch thick and use it to line the prepared tart pan. Prick the bottom of the pastry case, line it with baking parchment and fill with baking beans. Bake blind for about 20 minutes, until golden, then set on a wire rack and allow to cool.

Combine the raspberry jam and sherry and stir together, then smear the mixture over the base of the pastry case.

In a large mixing bowl, cream together the butter and sugar until light and fluffy. Add the beaten eggs, a little at a time, folding through thoroughly between each addition, then add the ground almonds and give it all a good stir. Spoon the batter into the pastry case and smooth level. Bake in the preheated oven for 20 minutes until it is all lovely and golden, like a Hollywood tan.

Remove from the oven and allow to cool. Once cool, remove the tart from the pan and decorate with raspberries and flaked/slivered almonds before serving.

Just a thought Seriously flappers, don't let anyone tell you that sherry is an old ladies' drink. Select yourself a Fino, a Manzanilla or an Oloroso. Serve with olives, almonds roasted in paprika and, of course, a slice of this wonderful tart.

the proof is
in the pudding

NAUGHTY NEW YEAR'S RESOLUTION

I don't know about you folks, but every Christmas brings liqueur chocolates and every New Year brings the same resolution... cut down on the chocolate. Well, out of sight, out of mind the good folks tell me. Hence, my Naughty New Year's Resolution creations were born. So empty out the cupboards and raid Grandma's secret stash because those leftover chocolate liqueurs have a date with your oven!

100 g/6½ tablespoons unsalted butter, softened

100 g/3½ oz. dark/bittersweet chocolate, roughly chopped

2 eggs, plus 2 egg yolks

80 g/⅓ cup plus 1 tablespoon caster/white sugar

100 g/¾ cup plain/all-purpose flour

20 g/3 tablespoons unsweetened cocoa powder

6 chocolate liqueurs

6 ramekin dishes, buttered

SERVES 6

BOOZE RATING

Preheat the oven to 190°C (375°F) Gas 5.

Very gently, melt the butter and chocolate in the microwave on short, low bursts or in a heatproof bowl set over a pan of barely simmering water.

In a large mixing bowl, whisk the eggs, egg yolks and sugar together until light and frothy, then gently fold in the melted chocolate and butter. Sift the flour and cocoa powder over the mixture and gently fold together.

Divide the batter equally between the ramekins. Gently push a chocolate liqueur into each ramekin and ensure that they are fully covered by the batter. Set the ramekins on a baking sheet and bake in the preheated oven for 10–12 minutes.

Take the dishes out of the oven – watch out as those ramekins will be hotter than the sidewalk on the 4th of July. Slide a sharp knife around the edge of each ramekin, then gently turn out each sponge onto a small plate to serve.

Just a thought You can sprinkle all sorts of goodies on these bad boys – here are just a few ideas: icing/confectioners' sugar; cocoa powder; glacé icing (mix up the icing/confectioners' sugar with a tiny drop of the same alcohol that was in the liqueur chocolate, or use a complimentary hooch); melt down a handful of chocolate liquers and drizzle this over the top; glacé/candied cherries; hulled and quartered strawberries; thick double/heavy cream.

SIDECAR CRÊPES

A Crêpe Suzette by another name, but what a name! – and I've added a few little twists and turns to keep it lively and lovely! Oh, the hearts that I've won and the tongues that I've loosened with these little devils. Absolutely the tip top, number 1, no doubting it, choice for a sinfully good night in with a few friends and some toe-tapping ragtime jazz.

4 eggs

100 g/¾ cup plain/all-purpose flour

½ teaspoon salt

2 tablespoons unsalted butter, melted

1 tablespoon caster/white sugar

120 ml/½ cup milk

2 teaspoons vanilla extract

FOR THE FILLING

400 g/14 oz. canned mandarin orange slices or 200 g/7 oz. canned mandarin slices plus 2 large blood oranges

100 ml/6½ tablespoons cup Cognac, Armagnac or bourbon

100 ml/6½ tablespoons Cointreau

icing/confectioners' sugar, to dust

SERVES 4

BOOZE RATING

Break the eggs into a large mixing bowl. Sift in the flour and salt, then add the melted butter and sugar and give everything a good whisk. Add the milk, vanilla extract and 120 ml/½ cup water and whisk for 3–4 minutes until you have a smooth, frothy batter, then put the mixture in the fridge for about an hour to chill.

Empty the mandarin oranges and their juice into a large bowl. If you're using blood oranges too, make sure that you not only peel them but remove as much pith as possible, then segment and roughly chop them. Add your Cognac, Armagnac or bourbon (for once in my life, I recommend picking just one of these bad boys and sticking with it), then add the Cointreau and allow to stand for at least an hour.

Remove the batter mix from the fridge and set to one side. Take a heavy-based frying pan and heat until, like you, it's smoking hot! Carefully ladle a spoonful of batter into the pan and quickly swirl the mix so that it creates a thin layer over the entire base. Try not to splash the mixture up the sides of the pan. Leave to cook over a high heat for 2–3 minutes on one side, then take a spatula and gently ease the edges of the crêpe free from the pan. Then flip it, toss it, turn it, whatever it is that you do, but get the other side cooking for a further 2–3 minutes. If needs be, you can always flip it back over to get an even light brown colour.

Lay the crêpe on a warm plate and add a tablespoon of the orange mix. Don't go too crazy or the crêpe won't roll! Roll the crêpe, drizzle a little of your orange juice mix over the top, dust with icing/confectioners' sugar and serve immediately.

TUACA TRAYBAKE

For the uninitiated amongst you, Tuaca is an Italian, brandy-based liqueur with soft citrus and vanilla notes... and for those of you in the know, it's an amber dream which softens your lens on life. Tuaca is the best, worst kept secret in cocktail shenanigans, so come on, join our family of Tuaca tantilizers.

400 g/14 oz. canned pineapple, drained, but hold onto that juice!

2 teaspoons ground ginger

75 ml/5 tablespoons Tuaca

freshly squeezed juice of
1 lemon

350 g/2¾ cups self-raising flour

2 teaspoons baking powder

225 g/2 sticks unsalted butter, softened

100 g/½ cup golden caster/natural cane sugar

100 g/½ cup dark muscovado sugar

4 eggs

100 g/3½ oz. preserved stem ginger, finely chopped

demerara sugar, for sprinkling

custard, to serve

a 20 x 27-cm/8 x 11-inch baking pan, greased and lined with baking parchment

SERVES 12–16

BOOZE RATING

Roughly chop the pineapple and put it in a bowl with 1 teaspoon of the ground ginger, 25 ml/1½ tablespoons of the reserved pineapple juice from the can, 50 ml/3½ tablespoons Tuaca and the lemon juice. Stir well and leave to stand for at least 30 minutes, then drain lightly and set aside.

Preheat the oven to 180°C (350°C) Gas 4.

In a separate mixing bowl, combine the flour, baking powder, butter, sugars, eggs, remaining 1 teaspoon ground ginger and the chopped stem ginger, and beat with an electric hand whisk until creamy.

Pour half the batter into the prepared cake pan and spread evenly, then spoon over half the drained pineapple and arrange evenly over the batter. Pour the remaining batter into the pan, spread evenly again, then arrange the remaining pineapple over the top. Sprinkle with demerara sugar and bake in the preheated oven for 45–50 minutes, until golden.

Once baked, remove the baking pan from the oven and prick the sponge all over with a skewer. Gently and slowly drizzle over the remaining Tuaca, then leave to cool for 10 minutes. Turn the sponge out of the pan and remove the baking parchment. Cut into squares and serve warm with custard.

Just a thought If custard is not your thing, here are a couple of alternative topping ideas: allow the cake to cool completely and smear a thin layer of glacé icing over the cake, followed by a sprinkling of pared lemon zest. Allow the icing to set, then cut into squares and serve. Or you could simply cut the cake into squares and serve with a dollop of cream cheese on top.

BANANA BAILEY'S CRUMBLE

These little guys are the perfect 'Quick, I'm hosting a dinner party and need a fabulous, domestic Goddess humdinger of a dessert!' dish. That and, of course, they are one of your five a day. They are so perky, in fact, that I have enough time to mix a jug of pre-dinner frivolity to really get the party shimmying. I recommend buying a few extra bananas and creating an alcoholic smoothie with crème de bananes, more Irish cream and plenty of crushed ice. Fabulous!

3 ripe bananas

100 ml/6½ tablespoons Bailey's Irish Cream

2 tablespoons clear honey

100 g/3½ oz. milk chocolate, roughly chopped

FOR THE CRUMBLE TOPPING

150 g/1 cup plus 2 tablespoons plain/all-purpose flour

100 g/6½ tablespoons unsalted butter, chilled and cubed

golden caster/natural cane sugar, for sprinkling

vanilla ice cream, to serve

6 small ramekin dishes

SERVES 6

BOOZE RATING

Preheat the oven to 190°C (375°F) Gas 5.

In a bowl, mash the bananas with the back of a spoon, then add the Bailey's and honey. Give the mixture a couple of good stirs, then divide between the ramekins (the mixture should come about two thirds of the way up the dish). Set aside while you make the crumble topping.

Put the flour and butter in a large mixing bowl and rub between your fingers until you have a crumbly texture. Cool hands and a cool head are required, so don't overwork the mixture.

Sprinkle the crumble topping over the Bailey's banana mixture, dividing it equally between the ramekins. Finally, sprinkle a little sugar on top of each crumble. Set the ramekins on a baking sheet and pop in the middle of the preheated oven to bake for about 12–15 minutes until the crumble is lightly golden. Serve immediately with a side order of vanilla ice-cream.

Just a thought If you're feeling a little more tropical, try substituting Malibu for the Bailey's and adding 75 g/¾ cup of desiccated/shredded coconut to the crumble topping mix.

BOOTLEG BREAD & BUTTER PUDDING

So I just can't decide...which version of this, one of my signature Kiki Bee dishes, do I confess to you? What's that? Amaretto, you holler? Amaretto it is. This is one of my most requested delectable dishes so it comes with a warning... be careful who you make this for, they will be camped out on your doorstep for forever more as this little darling is truly, love at first bite.

8–10 slices day-old panettone

50 g/3½ tablespoons butter, softened

4 fresh plums, pitted and sliced

100 g/⅔ cup roughly chopped almonds

300 ml/1¼ cups whole milk

250 ml/1 cup double/heavy cream, plus extra to serve

3 eggs

1 teaspoon vanilla extract

50 g/¼ cup golden caster/ natural cane sugar

75 ml/5 tablespoons amaretto

a large ovenproof dish, greased

SERVES 6–8

BOOZE RATING

Preheat the oven to 180°C (350°C) Gas 4.

Butter the panettone slices and sandwich them together in pairs, then cut each sandwich diagonally into 4 triangles. Arrange the bread triangles in rows in the dish and sneak some of the fresh plum slices between the layers, then sprinkle over half of the chopped almonds.

In a jug/pitcher, whisk together the milk, cream, eggs, vanilla, sugar and two thirds of the amaretto. Pour it over the bread and allow to soak for about 20 minutes.

Once the bread is good and sozzled, sprinkle over the remaining almonds and drizzle over the rest of the amaretto. Bake in the preheated oven for about 30–40 minutes. Serve warm with thick double/heavy cream.

Just a thought If you prefer, you can subsitute chopped prunes for the fresh plums, scattering them between the layers of bread. Or if, like me, you are a fickle flibberty jibbet, why not try mixing up the ingredients a little? Brioche and Cognac will have your guests 'ooh la la-ing.'

BELLINI COBBLER

Now this really is a Southern States classic and best enjoyed sitting on your porch, swinging on your chair whilst a handsome young man dressed in a pale linen suit reads Tennessee Williams to you. Failing that, sitting on your sofa watching *Gone with the Wind* will do just as well.

25 g/2 tablespoons unsalted butter

50 g/generous ⅓ cup plain/all-purpose flour

200 g/1 cup golden caster/natural cane sugar

1 teaspoon baking powder

a pinch of salt

150 ml/⅔ cup milk

1 x 247-g/9-oz. can peach halves, drained

50 ml/3½ tablespoons peach schnapps

50 ml/3½ tablespoons dry white wine or Martini

vanilla ice cream, to serve

a 27 cm x 17-cm/11 x 7-inch oval baking dish

SERVES 6–8

BOOZE RATING

Set the oven to 190°C (375°F) Gas 5.

Put the butter in the ovenproof dish and allow it to melt in the warming oven, being careful not to let it burn.

In a large mixing bowl, combine the flour, half of the sugar, the baking powder and the salt, then add the milk and gently stir to a smooth batter.

Remove the dish from the oven and pour the batter over the melted butter. Don't stir or fret with it at this point – just let it be.

Put the peaches in a saucepan with the remaining sugar, the schnapps and the wine and bring to the boil, stirring constantly, for 3–5 minutes. Strain the peaches (but hold onto that lovely liquor – nothing goes to waste in this bakery!) and arrange them over the batter. Put the dish in the preheated oven and bake for 25–30 minutes, until golden brown.

When you are ready to serve, warm the reserved schnapps and dry white wine, being careful not to let it boil, and drizzle this over each serving of cobbler. Serve with vanilla ice cream.

CHAMPAGNE COCKTAIL... NO TRIFLING MATTER

FOR THE CHAMPAGNE JELLY

40 g/3 tablespoons caster/white sugar

400 ml/1¾ cups Champagne (Cava, Prosecco or sparkling wine will work just as well)

3 gelatine leaves

100 g/3½ oz. sweet grapes, peeled and halved

FOR THE SPONGE LAYER

150 g/1 stick plus 2 tablespoons unsalted butter

100 g/½ cup caster/white sugar

2 large eggs, beaten

150 g/1 cup plus 2½ tablespoons self-raising flour

75 ml/5 tablespoons sweet white wine

FOR THE DECORATION

200 g/¾ cup double/heavy cream, whipped

a handful of peeled and halved grapes that have sat in a little sweet white wine

a 20 x 30-cm/8 x 12-inch baking pan, well greased

6 individual deep serving dishes

SERVES 6

BOOZE RATING

Baking is no trifling matter but just this once, let's pretend that it is. This is a great chic dinner party dessert. I mean, what's a party without jelly? Just play nicely with that cream... or naughty, if that works for you.

Put the sugar in a saucepan with 200ml/¾ cup water and warm over a gentle heat. Stir until all the sugar has dissolved, then quickly bring up to the boil. Reduce the heat and simmer for 3–5 minutes, then remove from the heat and set aside.

Put the Champagne in a large mixing bowl, add the gelatine leaves and leave them to soak for a few minutes, until the leaves are good and squidgy. Remove the leaves, give them a little shake and add them to your sugar syrup, then give it a whisk and a half – get that wrist moving, flapper! Once the leaves have dissolved, pour the syrup into the Champagne and give it another good whisk, then pop in the fridge for 50–60 minutes. Don't forget about it though – as it begins to thicken, stir through the peeled and halved grapes. Don't add them too early or they will all sink to the bottom and, well, no one wants a fruity bottom. Divide the jelly between the serving dishes and cover with cling film/plastic wrap. They'll need to chill for 4–6 hours before they are completely set, so this is the perfect time to make the cake... Preheat the oven to 180°C (350°C) Gas 4.

In a large mixing bowl, cream together the butter and sugar. Add the eggs and give it all a good stir so that you have a lovely creamy consistency. Sift the flour over the mixture and fold in. Pour the batter into your prepared baking sheet and bake in the preheated oven for 15–20 mins, until golden brown. Turn the cake out onto a wire rack and leave to cool.

Using your serving dishes as a guide, cut out rounds of cake that will fit into the dishes. Pop a round of cake into the top of each dish and drizzle a little of the sweet white wine over each one, dividing it equally between the dishes. Now add a healthy blob of whipped cream to the top of each trifle. Decorate with a few of the grapes and serve.

INDEX